The Beatles
A Life in Music

What was Beatlemania

John, Paul, George & Ringo

This is a FLAME TREE Book

FLAME TREE PUBLISHING
6 Melbray Mews
Fulham, London SW6 3NS
United Kingdom
www.flametreepublishing.com

First published 2022

22 24 26 25 23
1 3 5 7 9 8 6 4 2

ISBN: 978-1-83964-952-3
ebook ISBN: 978-1-83964-953-0

A copy of the CIP data for this book is
available from the British Library.

Printed and bound in the UK by Clays Ltd, Elcograf S.p.A

MIX
Paper from
responsible sources
FSC® C018072

The Beatles
A Life in Music

What was Beatlemania
John, Paul, George & Ringo

Hugh Fielder

Tony Bramwell
(Foreword)

UNOFFICIAL

**FLAME TREE
PUBLISHING**

Contents

Foreword

I first became friends with George Harrison in 1953. We lived close to each other and used to play Cowboys and Indians and other games that were allowed at the time – I still have a scar on my neck from a misfired arrow!

George was learning guitar and would come around to my house and learn songs from my family's record collection. I lost touch with him for a while, but met him again on a bus, when we were both headed to a dance at Litherland Town Hall. He was in a band playing there and I asked if I could carry his guitar so I could get in for free. I was astonished to see he was in this group called The Beatles, alongside Paul McCartney and John Lennon, two boys whom I also knew. They were so good and so exciting to see perform. I continued meeting up with them – and carrying things – until Brian Epstein became their manager and he asked me to work for him and The Beatles, which I did for their entire career.

The Beatles are still the most respected and lauded of any musicians and entertainers. Reissues of their recordings in new formats outsell most contemporary releases and open the group up to new audiences all the time. But, having known them from the very beginning, and having attended most of their shows over the years, I remember them most fondly as the little rock band they were before the world recognized them as The Fab Four or The Mop Tops. Nowadays, I find it fun to attend some of the tribute festivals, which attract thousands of people, and relive The Beatles experience all over again.

Tony Bramwell
Record promoter and former CEO of Apple Records

Four Ways The Beatles Changed The World

'If it hadn't been for The Beatles, there wouldn't be anyone like us around.'

Jimmy Page, Led Zeppelin

The Beatles were the first band to write all their hits. They changed the course of popular music history and the record industry. There are many ways they were revolutionary, but take these four for starters...

They Revolutionized Pop Music

Their songs were influenced by the American rock'n'roll they had been playing in the clubs of Liverpool, as well as Hamburg where they served their apprenticeship, along with emerging pop trends like Tamla Motown. They added their own individual and immediately identifiable style, however, which struck with a teenage generation looking for something they could call their own - resulting in a frenzied enthusiasm. The media called it Beatlemania.

They Opened The Flood Gates

In the wake of The Beatles' first flush of success, a host of other British bands jumped aboard the bandwagon. Liverpool bands in particular were tumbling over themselves - Gerry and the Pacemakers, The Searchers, Billy J. Kramer and the Swinging Blue Jeans. Out of London came The Rolling Stones, The Who, The Kinks, Small Faces, Manfred Mann and The Yardbirds. And it spread - The Spencer Davis Group from Birmingham, The Hollies from Manchester, The Animals from Newcastle, Them from Belfast ... Behind them were dozens more. Some even got lucky with a hit written by Lennon and McCartney.

They Conquered America

No British act had ever succeeded in America before The Beatles. EMI's US subsidiary Capitol Records didn't even bother to release their early records, but once they scored a No. 1 with 'I Want to Hold Your Hand', early in 1964, the speed at which The Beatles dominated the charts remains unsurpassed. At the beginning of April, they occupied all top five positions of the Billboard Hot 100. Their first American TV performance on *The Ed Sullivan Show* in February 1964 had a world record 73 million audience. For many US rock stars of the late-1960s and 1970s, that show was a pivotal moment in their career.

They Stayed Ahead Of The Game

Despite some lively competition, The Beatles remained ahead of the pack throughout their career. After their early pop phase – so prolific they were handing out songs to other bands like confetti – they pioneered the switch towards more reflective lyrics and sophisticated songwriting. They embodied the spirit of 1967 with their masterpiece *Sgt.*

Pepper's Lonely Hearts Club Band. They were at the front of the rollercoaster ride through the rest of the 1960s and although the end was inevitably messy, when they split up early in 1970, it really was the end of an era.

'I'm a melody freak and they

were the masters.'

Billy Joel

1957–59: That'll Be The Day

'The Beatles were the Mozart

of popular music. No one ever

equalled their extraordinary

output between 1963 and 1970.'

Tim Rice

The Beatles – Richard Starkey (Ringo Starr, born 7 July 1940), John Winston Lennon (9 October 1940), James Paul McCartney (18 June 1942) and George Harrison (24 February 1943) – were wartime babies, who were born and grew up in 1950s Liverpool, a major port that was still recovering from the bomb damage of the Second World War. They all moved house at least once as the city was rebuilt.

Meet The Beatles

McCartney and Harrison met as teenagers riding the same bus home from school, bonding over a shared love of skiffle, the latest pop craze to sweep Britain. McCartney met Lennon, who had formed a skiffle band called the Quarry Men, when they played a garden fete on 6 July 1957. He successfully auditioned for the band playing Eddie Cochran's 'Twenty Flight Rock' on Lennon's guitar (upside down because he was left handed) and impressed Lennon by knowing all the words. Harrison was still only 14 and had to wait until his 15th birthday in February 1958 before he could join.

From Quarry Men To Moondogs

Although they recorded their first demo in the summer of 1958 – a cover of Buddy Holly's 'That'll Be The Day' and a McCartney/Harrison song called 'In Spite Of All The Danger' – the Quarry Men, with Harrison on lead guitar and Lennon and McCartney playing rhythm, struggled to get gigs and hit a hiatus in early 1959 after Lennon's mother was killed by a speeding car (he'd never known his sailor father). But Lennon and McCartney hung out together and started writing songs, including 'One After 909' that would show up on The Beatles' final album, *Let It Be*, in 1970.

They resumed gigging later in the year without a bass player and with a succession of drummers (several of whom were driven away by Lennon's vicious temper), but they still managed to progress to the final of the *Star Search* competition in Manchester under the name Johnny & The Moondogs. Unfortunately, they ducked out of their final spot to catch the last train back to Liverpool.

1960: I'll Never Dance With Another

'We can't read music, sorry ... we

can play the Harry Lime Cha-Cha

which we've arranged ourselves ...'

Paul Mccartney

At the beginning of 1960, Lennon persuaded his art-school mate Stuart Sutcliffe to join the band on bass. He arrived with a stylish Hofner bass (that he couldn't actually play) and a new name for the band – The Beetles. This was soon expanded to The Silver Beetles by their first manager, Alan Williams, who got them gigs on the rough 'n' tough local dancehall circuit, a Scottish tour backing fellow Liverpool singer Johnny Gentle and a job providing the accompaniment for a stripper called Janice at an illegal strip club he'd opened.

From Beetles to Beatles and Best

By the summer, they were drummer-less once more, with McCartney having to fill in behind the kit. When Williams offered them a residency in Hamburg, Germany, if they could find a drummer, they began a frantic search. Just in time, they found Pete Best, who had limited experience, but was well-practised and, most important, available. The next day, 16 August, the band who had now settled on the name The Beatles, piled into Alan Williams's van and drove to Hamburg.

Hamburg Daze

Seven days a week, five hours a night (six on Saturday and Sunday), that was The Beatles' gruelling schedule for the next four months at the Indra Club and then the Kaiserkeller, where the owner exhorted them to 'Make show! Make show!'. Their set list featured rock'n'roll, rhythm and blues, pop, show tunes and even a couple of their own songs, notably 'I Saw Her Standing There'. They slept in a nearby cinema in a room behind the screen and lived on a diet of beer and amphetamines.

They were briefly joined by one of Liverpool's top bands, Rory Storm and the Hurricanes, whose drummer had recently renamed himself Ringo Starr. He took an instant shine to The Beatles, even playing with them at a recording session for the Hurricanes' bassist Lou Walters. None of the resulting acetates have survived, however. The Beatles' first Hamburg adventure ended in ignominy after they switched allegiance to the rival Top Ten Club, and the vengeful Kaiserkeller owner had Harrison deported for being underage, along with McCartney and Best for arson. Only Sutcliffe remained behind, with his girlfriend Astrid Kirchherr.

'It was all that work on various club stages in Germany that built up our beat.'

Paul McCartney

1961: Bring Back My Bonnie

'When we came back from

Germany, we were a wow!'

John Lennon

Back in Liverpool, The Beatles found that their Hamburg show quickly made them one of the hottest acts in town and they soon landed a residency at the Cavern Club. When their stand-in bassist quit, they decided to resolve the issue themselves and McCartney drew what was considered to be the short straw. In March, they returned to Hamburg for another three-month stint, getting reacquainted with

Sutcliffe and copying his leather-clad look for their stage outfits.

'Ain't She Sweet'

They also made their official recording debut as a backing band for Tony Sheridan. A rocked-up version of 'My Bonnie Lies Over The Ocean', retitled 'My Bonnie', got to No. 5 in the German charts, credited to Tony Sheridan and The Beat Brothers. During the session, they recorded two tracks by themselves - 'Ain't She Sweet' with Lennon on vocals, and the instrumental 'Cry For A Shadow' - which were buried in Polydor's vaults, but hurriedly retrieved a couple of years later when The Beatles became famous.

Epstein Meets The Beatles

That autumn, the band adopted the 'mop top' hairstyle, which would become their defining image, as Beatlemania broke. It was Sutcliffe's girlfriend, Astrid Kerchherr, who had first suggested the look and, after a few half-hearted attempts, they all took the plunge. All except Best, that is, who stubbornly hung on to his quiff, which he believed was vital to his pulling power.

In November, they met Brian Epstein. The manager of the record department at his father's electrical appliance store in the centre of Liverpool, he had been taking an interest in the growing Liverpool scene. He became intrigued by The Beatles after getting requests to track down Tony Sheridan's 'My Bonnie' single by fans. He checked them out one lunchtime at the nearby Cavern Club. 'They were fresh and they were honest and they had a sort of presence,' he recalled. He set up a meeting, at which he offered to manage them and promised to get them a record contract. He also set about making them more professional; no more scoffing jam butties onstage.

'I was excited about their prospects, provided some things could be changed ...'

Brian Epstein

1962: You Know I Love You

'An unusual group, not as rocky as most, with a tendency to play music.'

BBC Audition Assessment

On New Year's Day 1962, The Beatles set up their equipment at Decca Records' studio in London and ran through a 15-song set, including three of their own – 'Like Dreamers Do', 'Hello Little Girl' and 'Love Of The Loved' (none of which they ever released themselves but gave to other artists). They were not at their best, however, after a 10-hour drive through snow storms the previous day. Decca picked Brian Poole & The Tremeloes instead and Artists and Repertoire (A&R) Head, Dick Rowe, told Epstein that 'guitar groups are on their way out'.

Back to Liverpool and Hamburg

While Epstein began a dispiriting trek around the record companies trying to interest them in The Beatles, the band returned to Liverpool to find that they had topped the poll in the local Mersey Beat music paper. In April they travelled to Hamburg for a seven-week residency at the Star Club, but were devastated on their arrival to find that Stuart Sutcliffe had died of a brain haemorrhage a few days earlier, probably the result of a fight after a Beatles gig a year earlier.

EMI In! Ringo In! Best Out!

The gloom was lifted when the band received a telegram on 9 May from Epstein: 'Congratulations boys. EMI request recording session. Please rehearse new material.' On 9

June, The Beatles made their first visit to EMI's Abbey Road Studios, where they made demos of four songs of which 'Love Me Do' showed the most potential. But their producer, George Martin, told Epstein he was not convinced by Pete Best's drumming and would use a session drummer.This brought to a head a growing discontent with Best from the other three – and not just because he refused to get a Beatle haircut, although that was symptomatic of his attitude. In August, the others told Epstein to fire Best and hire Ringo Starr. It caused a local furore among the growing number of Beatles' fans and Ringo's first gig with them ended in fights, with Harrison getting a black eye. In contrast, Lennon's marriage to his pregnant girlfriend, Cynthia Powell, the following week was a deliberately low-key affair.

'Love Me Do'

Ringo was also an unknown quantity as far as George Martin was concerned. When The Beatles arrived at Abbey Road Studio to record their first single in September, he stuck with session drummer Andy White; Ringo was given a tambourine to bang. He was disconsolate, but it never happened again.

Martin also harboured doubts about whether 'Love Me Do' would be a hit and had sent the band a demo of 'How Do You Do It' by young songwriter Mitch Murray. The Beatles duly worked up a version of the song, but were clearly not over-enthusiastic about it and even Martin had to admit that 'Love Me Do' had more conviction about it.

In the end, 'How Do You Do It' was recorded using The Beatles' arrangement – by another Liverpool band, Gerry and The Pacemakers (the second band to be signed by Epstein), and shot to No. 1 early in 1963 – before The Beatles themselves reached the coveted spot.

Last Tango In Hamburg

'Love Me Do' was released on Parlophone Records on 26 October and climbed slowly up the charts, reaching a peak of 17 just after Christmas. Although it obviously sold well in Liverpool – Epstein was rumoured to have ordered 10,000 for his record store – the band were scarcely known beyond the city and although they appeared on a regional TV show for Granada in Manchester, national press and radio play was minimal.

The band themselves were not around much to promote 'Love Me Do', as they had to return to Hamburg for two more two-week residencies that had been agreed earlier. It was a distraction they could have done without and they were becoming less tolerant of their living accommodation - to the point where Lennon appeared at one show in his underpants with a toilet seat around his neck in protest. Back home, they got to support one of their biggest heroes, Little Richard, at the prestigious Liverpool Empire, which was some consolation.

'"Love Me Do" was our greatest philosophical song.... For it to be simple, and true, means that it's incredibly simple.'

Paul Mccartney

1963: If There's Anything I Can Do

'Man, those Beatles are fabulous!

If I hadn't seen them, I'd never

have dreamed they were white.'

Little Richard

Any doubts George Martin had about Lennon and McCartney's songwriting were dispelled by the recording session for The Beatles' second single. 'Please Please Me' had the fresh youthful vigour he had been hoping for and was laden with attractive musical hooks.

'Please Please Me'

Repaying his faith in them, the band adopted his suggestions for improving the song's commercial appeal. And this time EMI's promotion team got behind it; the group appeared on the influential *Thank Your Lucky Stars* ITV show on 11 January, the day it was released. The single made the Top 20 in early February and although some charts placed it at No. 1, it peaked at No. 2 in the most important Record Retailer chart.

The band embarked on the first of a succession of package tours around the country. They were bottom of a bill topped by child singing star Helen Shapiro, although as 'Please Please Me' climbed up the charts, so rose their billing, until they were closing the first half of the show. Lennon and McCartney offered Shapiro a song called 'Misery' that her management never even played to her.

A Hard Day's Work

On 11 February, the band recorded their first album – in one 13-hour session. As Paul McCartney recounts:

'We went into the studio at 10 in the morning, did one number, had a cup of tea, relaxed, did the next one, a couple of overdubs. And by about 10 o'clock that night, we'd done 10 songs and we just reeled out of the studio, John clutching his throat tablets.' George Martin wanted to catch the essence of their live set, from the briskly rocking 'I Saw Her Standing There' to the raucous 'Twist And Shout', by which time John Lennon's voice was completely shot.

Please Please Me was released on 22 March, just as The Beatles were finishing up their second package tour 'supporting' Chris Montez and Tommy Roe, although after the first night they closed the show. The album reached No. 1 after a couple of weeks and stayed there until it was replaced by their second album in November.

'From Me To You'

Released on 11 April, just as *Please Please Me* reached the top of the album charts, 'From Me To You' tightened The Beatles' grip on the charts. It took just two weeks to top the singles chart and stayed there for seven weeks.

Written on the Helen Shapiro tour bus between York and Shrewsbury, 'From Me To You' was accepted by George Martin rather than grabbed enthusiastically. But it did the job; it was identifiably Beatles from the opening seconds and laden with simple hooks and lyrics.

Getting access to vital radio airplay and TV exposure on the BBC – the country's only national broadcaster – became easier after The Beatles had crawled their way through a stodgy auditioning process. Producers and presenters found their cheeky wit and humour a pleasure to work with and, in addition to dedicated light entertainment shows, they found themselves on various children's shows, sometimes alongside a glove puppet or clown. The breakthrough came when they were given their own Tuesday teatime radio show, *Pop Go The Beatles*.

'She Loves You'

After another package tour – this time it was Roy Orbison who graciously declined to close the show – and a series of summer shows at seaside resorts around the country, The Beatles released their fourth single, 'She Loves

You', on 23 August with advance orders of 750,000. The gimmicky 'Whoooo' on the chorus with Lennon and McCartney shaking their mop tops together (inevitably provoking hysterical screams from the audience) was another idea from the Helen Shapiro tour bus. 'She Loves You' was the biggest selling single in Britain, until 1978 when it was surpassed by Paul McCartney and Wings' 'Mull Of Kintyre'.

That August they played their last show at the Cavern Club as it was becoming impossible to protect the band from their fans. As it was, Lennon had the sleeve of his jacket ripped off trying to get in. The Beatles had also become ambivalent about returning to Liverpool. Lennon said, 'Being local heroes made us nervous. We felt embarrassed in our suits. We were worried that our friends would think we had sold out. Which we had in a way.'

Beatlemania

On 13 October, The Beatles topped the bill of the country's most-watched TV entertainment show, *Sunday*

Night at the London Palladium, compered by Bruce Forsyth. Fans outside the Palladium spilled out on to the surrounding streets, and newspaper reports the following day contained the first mention of 'Beatlemania'. In fact, it had been going on for months. Getting the band in and out of theatres had become a logistical nightmare. And, once inside, they were trapped. Even the takeaway food they ordered needed a police escort. On stage, they were assailed by a barrage of screams that rendered them inaudible. The most reserved audience they had all year was at *The Royal Command Performance*, on 4 November, before the Queen Mother and Princess Margaret. They were not top of the bill, but they were certainly the most talked-about act. Lennon introduced 'Twist And Shout' by telling the people in the cheap seats to: 'Clap your hands. The rest of you rattle your jewellery.'

'This is what happens with fame.

This is celebrity. We thought,

"Well we'd better get on with it".'

Paul McCartney

With The Beatles

The Beatles' second album, *With The Beatles*, was a major leap forward, from the songs and production to the stylish black and white cover. The Lennon and McCartney songwriting partnership had taken another uplifting stride, notably on the opening trio of 'It Won't Be Long', 'All I've Got To Do' and 'All My Loving'. They were followed by George Harrison's first recorded song, 'Don't Bother Me'. There were also three covers from the little-known Tamla Motown label, plus the Broadway ballad 'Till There Was You'. Released on 22 November, *With The Beatles* replaced *Please Please Me* at No. 1 and stayed there for 21 weeks.

One week later, The Beatles released 'I Want To Hold Your Hand', their first international hit. It had started out as a rock-gospel song written by McCartney, with Lennon, in the basement of his girlfriend Jane Asher's house. But, at Abbey Road Studios, they added all kinds of musical tricks, from the deliberate stumble on the opening riff to the clever hand claps and the harmony crashes in the chorus, to turn it into something more ingenious.

1964: Money Can't Buy Me Love

'They've got everything over

there, will they want us too?'

Ringo On America

The Beatles made little impact in America during 1963. No British act had been successful in the US and EMI's American subsidiary Capitol had passed on the early Beatles' releases, leaving them to independent labels who lacked the resources to promote and market the band. Brian Epstein had flown to America in November 1963 to persuade Capitol to get behind 'I Want To Hold Your Hand' and the label eventually agreed to press up 200,000 copies for release in January 1964.

American Breakthrough

But they were overtaken by events. A Washington Radio DJ played the single in response to a listener request after his air-stewardess girlfriend brought it back from England. The response was immediate and overwhelming. He told his DJ mate in Chicago. Same thing. He told his DJ mate in St Louis.

Same thing. And so on, all over the country. Capitol hurriedly increased the pressing to a million and brought forward the release to Boxing Day 1963, giving kids a week to buy it before going back to school – by which time, they'd run out of copies.

America Conquered

When The Beatles landed in New York on 7 February, they were met at the airport by 5,000 screaming fans,

200 journalists waiting for a press conference and photographers dangling from forklift trucks trying to get pictures. That set the tone for their two-week visit; every hotel they stayed in was besieged by fans, with DJs and reporters making wild and ingenious plans to gain access to their inner sanctum.

'We've never seen anything like this before. Not even for kings and queens.'

Spokesman, JFK Airport, New York

The band played concerts at New York's prestigious Carnegie Hall and Washington's 10,000 capacity Coliseum, but the real purpose of their visit was to appear on *The Ed Sullivan Show*, America's most popular entertainment show. Their first performance has been described as a defining moment in American rock'n'roll history – 13½ moments, to be exact. The show's audience of 73.7 million was the largest in TV history. Alice Cooper,

Billy Joel, Joey Ramone, Tom Petty and Joe Walsh are just some of those who have recounted how the show changed their lives.

'... man, our tours were like

something else ...'

John Lennon

'Can't Buy Me Love'

No sooner had they got back from America than The Beatles had another single ready to go. It was George Martin's idea to adapt the chorus of 'Can't Buy Me Love' so that they could start the song with it. Like all their early singles, the message was clearly stated in the title (although an American journalist, desperate for an angle, argued that it was about prostitution), which deliberately included an 'I/you/me/we' pronoun for people to identify with.

Released on 11 April, 'Can't Buy Me Love' was an instant No. 1 on both sides of the Atlantic, adding to the remarkable domination of the American charts by The Beatles in the first half of 1964. After 'I Want To Hold Your Hand', those independent labels that had unsuccessfully released earlier singles put them out again and had massive hits. At the beginning of April, The Beatles held all Top 5 chart positions with 'Can't Buy Me Love', 'Twist And Shout', 'She Loves You', 'I Want To Hold Your Hand' and 'Please Please Me'.

A Hard Day's Night

In the midst of all this Beatlemania, the group worked on their first feature film. Lennon and McCartney wrote an entire album of songs for *A Hard Day's Night* during a three-week residency at the Paris Olympia, staying at the posh George V Hotel. Half of them were featured in the film, which was a simple mix of fiction and documentary that allowed The Beatles to play themselves – something they were getting good at.

Despite, or maybe because of the hectic shooting schedule, *A Hard Day's Night* (a remark Ringo made one evening, which was turned into a song by Lennon that was instantly recognizable from the opening chord) catches The Beatles at their most natural. Already under perpetual media scrutiny every time they stepped out, John, Paul, George and Ringo (as they were now colloquially known) carried on as normal on the film set.

'The picture adds up to a lot of fun, not only for the teenagers but for grown-ups as well. It's clean, wholesome entertainment.'

The *New York Daily News* reviews

A Hard Day's Night

John Lennon, meanwhile, couldn't stop multitasking. His book of jottings, *John Lennon: In His Own Write*, was recommended by *The Times Literary Supplement* 'for anyone who fears for the impoverishment of the English language'.

World Tour

In June, the first leg of The Beatles' world tour got off to a bad start when Ringo collapsed with tonsillitis and pharyngitis and was left behind. Hastily recruited session drummer Jimmy Nicol joined the band for shows in Europe and Hong Kong, where they failed to sell out two shows because the promoter was charging an average weekly wage for a ticket. Ringo rejoined the band in Australia, where the mayhem reached American levels – the difference being that the Australian police did not seem to think it was their responsibility to protect the band.

The American tour reached new heights of bedlam during 32 shows in 24 cities in 34 days. Their Kansas City hotel cut up their bed linen for sale at $3 a piece. At the Hollywood Bowl, it was their towels. They played their shows under a bombardment of jelly beans (George had foolishly mentioned they were his favourite sweets) and couldn't even hear themselves on the shoddy equipment provided. The arrival of Bob Dylan at their New York hotel with some marijuana was a welcome relief.

'I Feel Fine' / *Beatles For Sale*

The Beatles ended a tumultuous year with another single that was identifiable from the opening note – although it took a lot of effort to make the acoustic guitar feedback sound 'accidental'. It was John Lennon's song, although George Harrison's fiendishly difficult riff and ambitious solo carried it.

Beatles For Sale, released in time for Christmas, was the third Beatles album in a year and there were times when it showed. It was patched together over three months in between tours, concerts and various promotional activities. They even looked weary on the cover. There was a wistful, downbeat flavour to many of the songs – 'No Reply', 'I'm A Loser', 'Baby's In Black' – although they could still rouse themselves on 'Eight Days A Week' and the cheery ballad 'I'll Follow The Sun'. The half dozen covers they added to their eight new songs harked back to their Hamburg set list. In other medical news, Ringo had his errant tonsils removed and refused to sell them, despite many offers.

1965: Here I Stand Head In Hand

'I was actually crying out for help. Most people think it's just a fast rock'n'roll song. I didn't realize it at the time... It was my fat Elvis period.'

John Lennon

There was a change in the atmosphere when The Beatles gathered at Abbey Road in mid-February after a break, during which Ringo married his long-time girlfriend Maureen Cox, to record songs for their next film. And it wasn't just the exotic cigarettes they dabbled with either.

They'd already decided to follow the same schedule as *A Hard Day's Night* and write an album's worth of songs, picking the best for the film, but one year later, their songwriting had matured and they found writing to order restricting.

Looking For Help

There were other changes too: Lennon and McCartney had started writing separately more and collaborating less. Unusually, they both abandoned songs they had started recording – a sign of frustration. Nevertheless, they had a bunch of good songs ready by the time they headed off to the Bahamas and Switzerland for filming. A bigger budget meant better locations, although in fact these had largely been decided by the band's accountants, who were looking to offset a massive tax bill.

'Ticket To Ride'

Frustrations there may have been, but every single The Beatles released maintained their lead over the following pack – headed by The Rolling Stones, The Who, The Animals and The Kinks. 'Ticket To Ride', with its chiming guitar riff, anchored by in- your-face harmonies and Ringo's solid, rhythmic beat, was the heaviest Beatles song yet. And nobody paid much attention to Lennon's misogynistic lyrics.

The Beatles had two more uplifting experiences in the summer of 1965. They were awarded MBEs by the Queen (nominated by Prime Minister Harold Wilson, eager to attract young voters). There was predictable outrage from crustier members of the establishment and previous recipients, one of whom called the band 'vulgar nincompoops'.

'I thought you had to drive tanks and win wars to win the MBE.'

John Lennon

Lennon and Harrison also took their first LSD trip, courtesy of their dentist who should probably have told them first. He should also have dissuaded them from trying to drive home after they'd freaked out. They made it to Harrison's house in Esher, just. Lennon said, 'It was just terrifying but it was fantastic. George's house seemed to be like a big submarine and I was driving it'. Hold that thought, John.

'Yesterday'

Help! had its film premiere in July and was given a rough ride by the critics, the first time the band had faced adverse criticism. After some early visual gags, the plot (Ringo kidnapped by an evil cult leader) became increasingly threadbare, and then desperate as the story swerved from tropical beaches to ski slopes for no apparent reason. Even The Beatles' famed 'spontaneity' often looked forced.

The critics were kinder to the soundtrack album released the following month, particularly to a song tucked away on the second side of the album. 'Yesterday' featured McCartney alone on acoustic guitar and was backed by an unobtrusive string arrangement by George Martin. The song had been hanging around for a few months, while McCartney convinced himself that the tune had not been nicked, subconsciously or not, from anyone else. Once he had done so, it only remained to write the lyrics and improve the working title of 'Scrambled Eggs'.

Back In The USA

It had been more than five months since The Beatles had played live when they set off on a short European tour with concerts in France, Spain and Italy, where they had the unusual experience of playing to rows of empty seats, because the promoters were charging exorbitantly high ticket prices that effectively excluded their young fan base. Traditional Beatlemania was resumed in America in August when the band played a dozen stadium shows in 10 cities, starting at New York's Shea Stadium in front of some 56,000 fans.

The mayhem was temporarily suspended during a five-day break when they holed up in Beverley Hills and spent one night tripping with The Byrds and Peter Fonda, and another in strained, stilted conversation with Elvis Presley at his nearby Bel Air home. Things loosened up once the guitars came out, but then Lennon blew it by asking Elvis when he was going to start making rock'n'roll albums again.

Rubber Soul

The frustrations that had been apparent during the recording of *Help!* had disappeared when The Beatles settled into Abbey Road to make their next album. Freed from the constraints of writing songs to order (the next movie script would be summarily rejected), the band effectively took charge in the studio, controlling how they wanted their songs to sound. George Martin's role was to translate their musical thoughts and ideas in the studio and make the songs happen. He wasn't short of his own ideas either; his baroque piano solo on 'In My Life' was a masterstroke.

The songs reflected their growing maturity. Lennon was getting more personal on 'Norwegian Wood' ('I was trying to write about an affair without letting my wife know I was writing about an affair') and 'Nowhere Man'. McCartney showed he could be musically complex and lyrically saucy on 'Drive My Car'. And Harrison was starting to perfect a style of his own on 'If I Needed Someone'. Released in December, *Rubber Soul* was a watershed moment for The Beatles.

> *'We were just getting better, technically and musically, that's all. Finally we took over the studio.'*
>
> John Lennon on *Rubber Soul*

'We Can Work It Out' / 'Day Tripper'

Yet another innovation from The Beatles was the first double A-sided single. Released at the same time as *Rubber Soul* (and the same day they started what would be their last British tour), it was assumed the radio would prefer the more commercial, riff- driven 'Day Tripper', but instead most DJs opted for the quirkier 'We Can Work It Out', with its harmonium drone and sudden switch into waltz time.

A film of The Beatles lip-synching the song was made for television and can fairly claim to be the world's first pop video – for the world's first double A-sided No. 1. The only downside to a satisfying Beatles Christmas was the appearance of Lennon's long-lost father, who crawled out of the woodwork and into the welcoming arms of the media, who encouraged his embarrassing attempts to reunite with his son. But as Lennon later said, 'I didn't want to see him. I was too upset about what he'd done to me and my mother. But he sort of blackmailed me in the press.'

1966: Dirty Story Of A Dirty Man

'Christianity will go. It will

vanish and shrink. I needn't

argue about that. I'm right and

I will be proved right. We're

more popular than Jesus now.

I don't know which will go first:

rock'n'roll or Christianity.'

John Lennon

At last, the incessant, hectic schedule The Beatles had endured for three years began to ease up. They paused for breath at the beginning of 1966. George Harrison married his girlfriend Patti Boyd, Paul McCartney tried writing a song under a pseudonym ('Woman') to see if it was a hit (it was) and John Lennon played with his new reel-to-reel tape recorder, inadvertently threading a tape the wrong way into the spool and discovering some interesting 'backwards' sounds. He used the effect on the first song the band recorded when they went back into the studio in March, 'Tomorrow Never Knows'.

Lennon Causes Controversy

But there were hidden dangers; when Lennon gave an interview to the *London Evening Standard*, he spoke about religion and mentioned that The Beatles were 'more popular than Jesus now'. The remark caused no raised eyebrows in Britain, but, in America, Christian groups seized on the remark to create a 'blasphemy' scandal. As the furore spread, radio stations started banning Beatles records and those who had been buying them by the million were now urged to destroy them.

'That's me in my Tibetan Book of the Dead period. I took one of Ringo's malapropisms as the title ... to take the edge off the heavy philosophical lyrics.'

John Lennon on 'Tomorrow Never Knows'

'Paperback Writer' / 'Rain'

The Beatles continued with their pioneering double A-sided single format in May, but this time, McCartney's rocker 'Paperback Writer', with its glorious electronically enhanced a capella chorus, pounding beat and strident guitars, won out easily over Lennon's stoned dirge 'Rain', enhanced by more backwards tapes. Again, the band made promotional films for use on TV; however, instead of a mimed performance, they took a stroll around Chiswick House in west London and left it to director Michael Lindsay-Hogg to make two early pop videos with rhythmic editing, slow motion and other tricks.

In May, the band also played what was their last British concert at the Wembley Empire Pool, headlining the NME Poll Winners Concert over The Rolling Stones, Cliff Richard & the Shadow, Small Faces, Dusty Springfield, The Who, Roy Orbison and The Walker Brothers. The Beatles' 15-minute set featured 'I Feel Fine', 'Nowhere Man', 'Day Tripper', 'If I Needed Someone' and 'I'm Down'. A ticket for the North Upper Tier was 25 shillings (that's £1.25 to you).

'Butcher' Sleeve

As the furore over Lennon's 'Beatles more popular than Jesus' quote raged on in America, the band narrowly avoided a second disaster when their US-only album *Yesterday And Today* was abruptly recalled from distribution depots on the eve of its release. The cover picture featured the band in white butchers' coats draped with pieces of raw meat and dismembered dolls. Capitol hastily prepared a new cover - a bland, inoffensive band shot - for the 750,000 albums already pressed. The handful of original covers that survived are now worth their weight in gold.

In June, the band headed to the Far East for concerts in Japan (where they were confined to their hotel for four days) and the Philippines, where they were 'kidnapped' by the military for various receptions, missing a reception organized by the First Lady Imelda Marcos. In a fury, Marcos withdrew their security and the band had a harrowing journey to the airport. They were then imprisoned on their plane until they handed over their concert fees on various trumped-up charges.

Revolver

Revolver marks the full emergence of The Beatles as a studio band – they brought in their songs and then worked on them collectively. Lennon and McCartney's songwriting was now diverging; McCartney was heading deeper into melody and soul with 'Here There And Everywhere' and 'Got To Get You Into My Life', while Lennon was heading deeper into his own head with 'She Said She Said' and 'Tomorrow Never Knows'. Harrison's confidence was growing on the strident, sardonic 'Taxman' and his first sitar song, 'Love You To'.

Meanwhile, producer George Martin provided the guidance, the encouragement and, crucially, the discipline. For many, *Revolver* remains the perfect Beatles album. Released in August, its diversity was best illustrated on the single they lifted from it. McCartney's 'Yellow Submarine' nursery rhyme was given to Ringo to warble, while John clanged bells, blew bubbles in a bucket and strutted around like a demented sailor. 'Eleanor Rigby' was another shaft of McCartney brilliance; a wistful lament made sublime by George Martin's double string quartet arrangement.

Third And Final Us Tour

Three days after *Revolver* came out, The Beatles arrived for their third American tour to find the blasphemy controversy going strong. Radio stations were still banning Beatles' records and Christian groups were organizing ritual burnings of them. Although as Harrison pointed out, 'They've got to buy them before they can burn them.' In vain, Lennon issued an abject apology and pointed out that he had been misunderstood, not to mention widely misquoted.

The 14-city tour was a tense, nervous affair with the band now trapped in their hotels by protests and death threats. When somebody let off a firecracker at the Memphis Mid-South Coliseum, the band were visibly shaken. Even the rain seemed to follow them around their stadium shows. The last show, on a foggy, windy night at San Francisco's Candlestick Park, was typical; the 42,000 capacity stadium was two-thirds full and The Beatles played their 11-song set (nothing from *Revolver*) in just over half an hour, behind a six-foot fence ringed by police, with an armoured car standing by, engine running.

'On our last tour people kept bringing blind, crippled and deformed children into our dressing room and [saying] "Go on, kiss him. Maybe you'll bring back his sight."'

John Lennon

The End Of The Beginning

When The Beatles announced in November that they would no longer play concerts – a decision made easy by the misery of their American tour – many people assumed they were splitting up and band obituaries started appearing in the press. The band themselves had scattered; Lennon to Spain to film *How I Won the War*, Harrison to India to study sitar with Ravi Shankar, and McCartney to write the film score for *The Family Way* (with a little help from George Martin).

When they reconvened at Abbey Road in November, there was not a mop top in sight; they now had individual hairstyles and their clothes were becoming increasingly garish as they took advantage of the burgeoning 'Swinging London' scene. They also had plenty of songs to work on and a renewed enthusiasm now that they had taken themselves off the treadmill.

On 9 November, Lennon, now sporting 'granny' glasses, went to the preview of an exhibition, Unfinished Paintings and Objects, at the Indica Gallery in London by Japanese artist Yoko Ono. 'She came up and handed me a card that said "Breathe".'

1967: Nothing To Get Hung About

'...we were a little intimidated by the idea of making "The new Beatles album". ... So ... I got the idea ... that we shouldn't record it as 'The Beatles'. Mentally we should approach it as another group of people entirely...'

Paul McCartney on *Sgt. Pepper*

The Beatles paved the way for their next masterpiece with a ground-breaking double A-sided single in February, featuring two contrasting nostalgic visits back to Liverpool.

'Penny Lane' / 'Strawberry Fields Forever'

McCartney strode gaily down 'Penny Lane' beneath 'blue suburban skies', nodding at the people and places, while a trumpet spiralled into the stratosphere. Lennon meanwhile, in 'Strawberry Fields Forever', took a trip (in every sense) back to a childhood haunt in a mesmerizing collage of atmospheric lyrics, mysterious mutterings, heavy insistent drumming, surreal strings and trumpets, fade-outs, fade-ins and, of course, backwards tapes. It was the first Beatles single not to get to No. 1 since 'Love Me Do' was thwarted by Engelbert Humperdinck's 'Release Me'. But The Beatles didn't care.

The band continued to reject film scripts that tried to cast them as the band that had made *Help!*, although they allowed maverick playwright Joe Orton to write a script that involved cross dressing, murder, group sex and gay references. It even had a title, *Up Against It*, but that was as far as it got.

Sgt. Pepper's Lonely Hearts Club Band

On 1 June, the music world paused to absorb the tapestry of delights that was *Sgt. Pepper's Lonely Hearts Club Band*. It became the soundtrack to the fabled Summer of Love, as fans devoured the galaxy of nuances and effects in each song, from the eager anticipation of the audience at the start to the final babble on the run-out groove. The clever segues between each song meant that there were no bands between the tracks, so each side of the album was one continuous track. This made it difficult for the BBC to ban the vivid 'Lucy In The Sky With Diamonds' and the monumental 'A Day In The Life' for perceived drug references, but they did their best.

The cover of *Sgt. Pepper* was as ground-breaking as the music. British pop artist Peter Blake photographed the band in their *Sgt. Pepper* day-glo military outfits, surrounded by cutouts of 70 or so of their heroes, arranged around them like a school photo, including their former mop-top selves. The Beatles' name was spelled out below in a floral arrangement.

'All You Need Is Love'

When Paul McCartney admitted that he had taken LSD in an interview with *Life* magazine in June, he provoked a media frenzy. In a filmed interview broadcast on the ITN evening news, he explained that he was simply being honest and that the media were responsible for spreading the story and the hysteria. A few weeks later, a full-page advertisement appeared in *The Times*, calling for the decriminalization of cannabis, signed by writers, Nobel prize-winning scientists, politicians – and all four Beatles.

The BBC had asked The Beatles to represent Britain in a pioneering show in June. *Our World* linked 14 countries across five continents by satellite. Lennon wrote 'All You Need Is Love', which they performed at Abbey Road Studios with a 13-piece orchestra and a celebrity backing vocals chorus that included Mick Jagger, Keith Richards, Marianne Faithfull, Eric Clapton and Keith Moon. They were surrounded by flowers and balloons, and placards that translated the song title into different languages. Not surprisingly, 'All You Need Is Love' was a worldwide No. 1 hit when it was released the following month.

Meditating with the Maharishi

Given The Beatles' extraordinary journey over the last five years, it was not surprising that they sought to make some sense of it all. When George Harrison's wife Pattie told them about the Indian spiritual guru Maharishi Mahesh Yogi they were all interested enough to attend a lecture he gave in London about transcendental meditation. They were so impressed, they immediately signed for up a weekend seminar he was holding in Bangor, North Wales. They stayed in student accommodation with the Maharishi's followers and a few journalists who also appeared to have taken up an interest in transcendental meditation.

It was while The Beatles were in Bangor that their manager Brian Epstein was found dead in his London house on 27 August from an overdose of sleeping pills. He was 32 years old. An inquest later ruled his death was accidental. The Beatles, in their meditative state, were barely able to comprehend the news. The Maharishi told them that Epstein's death in the physical world was 'not important'.

'Paul made an attempt to carry on as if Brian [Epstein] hadn't died by saying, "Now, now, boys, we're going to make a record"... And that's when we made Magical Mystery Tour.'

John Lennon

Magical Mystery Tour

In the wake of Epstein's death, The Beatles decided to manage themselves. And having turned down all film proposals, they elected to make their own movie. McCartney came up with the idea of a *Magical Mystery*

Tour and they hired a coach, painted it in psychedelic patterns and set off to the West Country with a bunch of actors and friends. There was no script, just an assortment of ideas. Likewise, the filming was spontaneous, although most of it was never used. The coach's progress was also slow as it had difficulty negotiating the narrow country lanes and was being followed by a posse of journalists.

There was a similar lack of focus when it came to recording the songs for *Magical Mystery Tour*. The songs themselves were certainly up to The Beatles' current creative standards – particularly Lennon's dense, epic 'I Am The Walrus', which fell foul of the BBC's censors when they heard the word 'knickers'. But apart from the title track, they did not appear to have any relationship to the film.

Apple To The Core

The Beatles had set up Apple Corps to manage their affairs after Epstein's death. The first venture was the Apple Boutique fashion store in Baker Street, London, which was decorated inside and out with suitably psychedelic designs. Turnover was high, but not much money flowed through the tills and the boutique closed suddenly eight months later, giving away all its remaining stock.

The Beatles ended 1967 with a Christmas No. 1. McCartney's cheery 'Hello Goodbye' was inconsequential but addictive. Lennon hated it. The BBC also managed to ban the accompanying promotional film by claiming that it broke Musicians Union rules on miming.

Magical Mystery Tour had its British premiere on Boxing Day on BBC TV to an audience of some 15 million, most of whom were left bemused as they tried to comprehend the non-existent plot. Not even the music could save it. It didn't help that the film had been shot in colour but screened in black and white because the BBC hadn't yet switched to colour.

'We went out to make a film and nobody had the vaguest idea what it was about.'

Neil Aspinall on *Magical Mystery Tour*

1968: Let Her Into Your Heart

'When John hooked up with Yoko

... it was kind of obvious that

there could be no looking back.'

Paul McCartney

In mid-February, The Beatles and their wives (and McCartney's now-fiancé Jane Asher) decamped to Rishikesh in India to attend the Maharishi's initiator training course at his ashram. Other initiators included Donovan, Beach Boy Mike Love and actress Mia Farrow. Ringo and Maureen missed their children and their bacon sandwiches and returned home after 10 days. Paul and Jane lasted another couple of weeks, but George, Pattie, John and Cynthia stuck it out until mid-April, when rumours that the Maharishi had made less-than-transcendental advances to some female initiators diminished their faith.

Productivity At The Ashram

The musical bonus was the number of songs they wrote whiling away the time at the ashram. They'd also recorded another single before they left, 'Lady Madonna'. McCartney returned to his roots, pounding out a Fats Domino-style boogie on the piano and singing through cupped hands at one point. But while Britain lapped up the nostalgia and sent it to No. 1, the Americans were less impressed and it peaked at No. 4.

Apple Pie

Back in the material world, The Beatles set about turning Apple Corps into a multifaceted operation. 'A kind of Western communism,' as McCartney put it. As well as managing The

Beatles' affairs, Apple set up a record label, signing Mary Hopkin and James Taylor. Other divisions included Apple Publishing, Apple Films, Apple Electronics and Apple Retail. Launched with fanfare in London and New York, Apple attracted thousands of applicants, from eager singers to madcap inventors. But dealing with the avalanche of demo tapes and wacky ideas seemed to depend on the whim of whichever Beatle happened to be around. And they could be very whimsical.

Meanwhile, John Lennon was going through a profound change in his life. Having confessed his serial adultery to an unsuspecting Cynthia on the flight back from India, he was increasingly drawn to Yoko Ono. One evening in May, when Cynthia was away, he invited Yoko over to hear his tapes. And then they made one together. 'It was midnight when we started *Two Virgins* and it was dawn when we finished. And then we made love at dawn. It was very beautiful.'

White And Yellow

When The Beatles gathered at George Harrison's house at the end of May to run through their songs, it was soon apparent that they had enough for a double album. Even

Ringo had written one. But when they started recording at Abbey Road, the atmosphere became strained, not least because John Lennon had Yoko Ono glued to his side in clear breach of the protocol that only the four Beatles should be in the studio. Paul McCartney's attempts to lead the group didn't help either. Lennon and McCartney even started working in separate studios, although they all crammed into a tiny box room to record 'Yer Blues'.

To the public, The Beatles were still in their post-*Sgt. Pepper* glow, an image reinforced by the *Yellow Submarine* animated movie. The full-length cartoon was awash with psychedelic day-glo, using recent Beatles tracks to bolster a silly story of Blue Meanies, Nowhere Men and Apple Bonkers set in Pepperland. And it held a charm for children of all ages. The Beatles themselves had almost nothing to do with it, although they made a cursory appearance at the end and dusted off four previously discarded songs for the film.

'Hey Jude'

The Beatles' first release on their own Apple Records on 30 August became their biggest-selling single. After Cynthia

Lennon instituted divorce proceedings against John, Paul McCartney was driving to see her (the only Beatle to show support) and son Julian, with whom he'd always been close, when he wrote the song. It was just two verses, a middle section and a long fade-out. But in the studio, the song took on anthemic qualities, especially during the epic, orchestra-enhanced finale. Worldwide sales topped 8 million.

Relations between the band in the studio had continued to deteriorate, however, and on 20 August, Ringo, the most easy-going Beatle, suddenly quit after fluffing a drum fill and being castigated by Paul. He flew to the Mediterranean and stayed on Peter Sellers' yacht, writing 'Octopus's Garden' one day, after turning down squid for lunch. He returned two weeks later after receiving a telegram saying, 'You're the best drummer in the world. Come home.' He found his kit festooned with flowers.

Going Solo

Recording sessions for the next Beatles album dragged on through the autumn amid tensions. George Harrison and John Lennon also occupied themselves with solo projects and Harrison produced the first album on Apple

Records in November, although he didn't play or sing on it. *Wonderwall Music* was a bland Indian-themed soundtrack to a voyeuristic 'art' movie starring Jane Birkin that barely surfaced before vanishing.

Lennon's soundtrack to his first night with Yoko, entitled *Unfinished Music No. 1: Two Virgins*, stirred up a mighty controversy with its cover featuring a full-frontal nude picture of the pair. It was sold in a plain brown wrapper, but that didn't stop New York police raiding warehouses in search of it. Intrepid listeners were confronted by bird calls, gastric juices (in stereo) squealing, a pub piano and tape effects. It was a busy time for Lennon. In addition to getting busted for cannabis with Yoko, he formed the one-off Dirty Mac with Eric Clapton and Keith Richards, and did a turn at *The Rolling Stones' Rock And Roll Circus*, playing 'Yer Blues'. Unfortunately, the show remained unseen for the next 22 years (the Stones withheld it, believing their own performance lacking).

The Beatles (The White Album)

After a mammoth mixing and sequencing session, *The Beatles* - or *The White Album*, as everyone called it

- was released at the end of November. It was the most diverse album they ever made. The contrast between Lennon's growing iconoclasm ('Glass Onion', 'Happiness Is A Warm Gun', 'Yer Blues', 'Sexy Sadie', 'Revolution 1') and McCartney's eclecticism ('Blackbird', 'Back In The USSR', 'Ob-la-di Ob-la-da', 'Honey Pie') was even more pronounced, while Harrison's contributions included the epic 'While My Guitar Gently Weeps' that featured an (uncredited) solo from Eric Clapton. They played on each other's songs like session musicians rather than bandmates. Critics who argued that it should have been trimmed down to a single album missed the point; it needed that sprawling chaos in order to make its point.

The pure white cover with 'The BEATLES' embossed on the front (the first five million copies were individually numbered), and its fold-out lyric sheet and photographs were yet another innovative design to match the album's contents.

'A lot of the recordings, they

would have a basic idea and then

they would have a jam session to

end it. Which sometimes didn't

sound too good.'

George Martin on *The White Album*

1969: Protected By A Silver Spoon

'You've been playing on the

roofs again and you know your

momma doesn't like it. She's

gonna have you arrested.'

Paul Mccartney ad-libs during 'Get

Back' at the rooftop concert

January found The Beatles on a sound stage at Twickenham Studios, filming rehearsals for a back-to-basics album and movie. But the tensions that had dogged *The White Album* soon reappeared, this time caught on camera. The songs were in short supply and the playing was uninspired.

Let It Be Sessions

George Harrison walked out after rows with Lennon and McCartney, and when he returned, they agreed to relocate to Apple's brand new basement studio – except that the 72-track console promised by Lennon's technical 'guru', the so-called 'Magic' Alex, had not materialized. He hadn't even made provisions to run cables from the studio to the control room. They ended up borrowing a couple of four-track machines from Abbey Road. In an attempt to lighten the atmosphere, the band drafted in keyboard player Billy Preston, who'd been visiting Apple in search of a record deal. The Beatles had known him back in 1962 when he was playing with Little Richard. Lennon and McCartney also remembered and revived a song they'd written around that time called 'One After 909'. Afterwards, they shelved the tapes while they decided what to do with them.

The 'Rooftop' Concert

A long-running, inconclusive debate about where and, even, if The Beatles would play a live show for their movie was suddenly resolved on 30 January. Their equipment was set up on the roof of Apple's Savile Row HQ and the band played an impromptu 42-minute lunchtime concert that reverberated around the streets below. As a crowd gathered, the police arrived to stop the show, but were stonewalled by the road crew until the set finished. At this point Lennon said, 'I'd just like to say "thank you" on behalf of the group and ourselves and I hope we passed the audition.' It was their last public performance.

Beneath The Beatles' feet as they played, Apple Corps was about to get a shake-up. A remark by Lennon a few weeks earlier that Apple's largesse was driving The Beatles towards bankruptcy had brought pugnacious New York lawyer Allen Klein scurrying over to London. He'd previously untangled The Rolling Stones' financial affairs (while appropriating their back catalogue for himself). He was welcomed by Lennon, who persuaded Harrison and Ringo, but not McCartney, who brought in his new American girlfriend Linda Eastman's lawyer father instead. It was about to get messy.

'He's alright if you like that kind of thing.'

Mick Jagger telling The Beatles about Allen Klein

Two Weddings and a Bust

On 12 March, Paul McCartney married New York photographer Linda Eastman at London's Marylebone Register Office after a year-long romance. (He had quietly broken off his engagement to Jane Asher earlier.) The reception was held at the Ritz, where guests included Princess Margaret and Lord Snowden. George Harrison was unavoidably delayed after he and Pattie were busted at their Esher home. Harrison later claimed in court that the police evidence was planted and they'd missed his actual stash.

John Lennon and Yoko Ono were also free to marry after their respective divorces came through, although their nuptials involved more shenanigans. Plans to marry aboard a cross-channel ferry were abandoned. Instead, the couple flew to Gibraltar for the ceremony and then to Amsterdam, where they invited the media to their honeymoon suite at the Hilton for a week-long 'Bed-In For Peace' in their pyjamas. The media duly relayed the message.

Rumours of The Beatles' imminent demise were quelled in April with the single 'Get Back', the first track to be salvaged from the *Let It Be* sessions. The McCartney rocker took them to the top of the charts on both sides of the Atlantic.

'The Ballad Of John And Yoko'

Just six weeks after 'Get Back', The Beatles released another single, 'The Ballad Of John And Yoko'. It was John's comment on his recent shenanigans, but it was also a rare and (given their growing business conflicts) unlikely Lennon/McCartney collaboration. In fact, they were the only performers, John playing guitars and Paul playing bass, piano and drums. In America, the blasphemy lobby seethed at the word 'Christ' and the phrase 'They're gonna crucify me'.

The Lennons weren't done yet though. After a brief 'Bed-In For Peace' in the Bahamas, where it was too hot and humid, they diverted to the Queen Elizabeth Hotel, Montreal, Canada. On 1 June, with an array of guests that included LSD guru Timothy Leary, singer/comedian Tommy Smothers, singer Petula Clark, a local rabbi and members of the Radha Krishna Temple, they recorded 'Give Peace A Chance' on some borrowed equipment. Released in July as the first single by the Plastic Ono Band, the song quickly became an anthem that reverberated around the world, politically and musically.

Abbey Road

With the fate of the *Let It Be* tapes unresolved, McCartney persuaded the others that they should make another album and 'go out on a high note'. George Martin agreed to produce them, provided it was done 'the way we used to'. The four of them temporarily set aside their business and personal disputes, and focused on making one more album. Sessions began in early July. McCartney had plenty of songs, Harrison had a few, but Lennon was struggling to get back into Beatle mode, although he did come up with the album's sardonic opener, 'Come Together'.

Harrison's two contributions, the genial 'Something' (that became his most-covered song) and the sweet, shimmering 'Here Comes The Sun' were the album's standout tracks. But it was the 15-minute suite of McCartney songs towards the end, briskly edited together, that brought the album to its delicious climax. If *Abbey Road,* released in late September, had indeed been The Beatles' last album, then it would have achieved exactly what McCartney and the others wanted. But it wasn't.

Lennon Breaks The Deadlock

Whatever harmony The Beatles had summoned up during the making of *Abbey Road* did not extend beyond the studio, where the turmoil of sorting out their financial affairs was dragging them down. Allen Klein had secured a better record deal and had taken a chainsaw to the overgrown Apple tree, but he was unable to prevent the band's publishing from falling into corporate hands.

Returning from a hastily arranged show in Toronto with the Plastic Ono Band, Lennon decided to act. 'It came to a point where I had to say something. So I said, "The group's over.

I'm leaving".' But he agreed to say nothing publicly for the time being. Instead, he released *The Wedding Album*, which mainly consisted of John and Yoko repeating each other's names in as many different ways as possible, the Plastic Ono Band's *Live Peace In Toronto* concert and the harsh, harrowing single, 'Cold Turkey'.

McCartney retreated to his Scottish farm and initially missed the 'Paul Is Dead' rumour that swept America. His every denial simply encouraged the conspiracy theorists. Ringo started recording his own album and George played on his friends' albums, and was even enticed back on stage with Eric Clapton and American band Delaney & Bonnie.

1970: Speaking Words Of Wisdom

'I for one am very proud of the Beatle thing. People you meet on the street say you gave so much happiness to so many people. I don't think that's corny.'

Paul McCartney

On 3 January, McCartney, Harrison and Ringo (Lennon was in Denmark) gathered at Abbey Road to record

Harrison's 'I Me Mine' that they had rehearsed during the *Let It Be* sessions a year earlier, but not recorded. It was the last official Beatles recording session.

Enter Phil Spector

When Lennon and Ono returned from Demark, they recorded a new Plastic Ono Band single, 'Instant Karma', which featured Harrison on guitar and was produced by the legendary Phil Spector. Impressed by his sound, the band (minus McCartney) gave him the *Let It Be* sessions to work on. The band had already rejected two versions of the album before Spector set to work in his inimitable fashion. However, Lennon and Harrison did not tell McCartney what they had done and he remained unaware, despite working on his solo album in the studio next door.

Meanwhile, the song 'Let It Be', another McCartney anthem with a gospel flavour courtesy of Billy Preston's organ fills and Harrison's guitar solo played through the organ's Leslie speaker, had already been earmarked as the next Beatles single and was released in March before Spector could get his hands on it.

'Yes, I was in the Beatles. Yes,

we made some great records

together. Yes, I love those boys.

But that's the end of the story.'

Ringo Starr

McCartney Announces Split

McCartney completed his first solo album around the same time Spector finished remixing *Let It Be*. When McCartney heard what Spector had done, he was appalled, particularly by the 'schmaltzy' strings that had been layered on to 'The Long And Winding Road'. He was also furious with his bandmates for going behind his back. But Lennon was unrepentant: 'He [Spector] was given the shittiest load of badly recorded shit with a lousy feeling to it and he made something of it.'

The final insult for McCartney came when he was asked to change the release date of his solo album in order to accommodate *Let It Be*. In a press release that accompanied his self-titled album in April, he publicly announced that The Beatles had broken up, citing 'personal differences, business differences, but most of all because I have a better time with my family'. Asked if he could envisage the Lennon/McCartney songwriting partnership becoming active again, he replied, 'No'.

Let It Be

When *Let It Be* was released on 8 May it sparked a debate about whether Phil Spector's production had saved or ruined the album. But the real problem was that, apart from the title track and 'Get Back', the quality of the songs was below the usual Beatles standard. McCartney exacted a measure of revenge in 2003 when he released *Let It Be... Naked* that removed Spector's production and went back to the original tapes, even changing some of the tracks.

As for the film, after a premiere (which none of the band attended) it was given a limited cinema release before disappearing. Its depiction of a band essentially breaking up was not the intention.

The Beatles' split became official at the end of 1970 when McCartney sued the others to dissolve the partnership. But the case dragged on until 1975 by which time Lennon, Harrison and Ringo were suing Allen Klein who was also suing them.

Epilogue

There were occasional rumours of a Beatles reunion throughout the 70s, usually when a promoter offered a preposterous sum of money for them to reform. But there's no evidence that any of the offers were taken seriously. However, they frequently contributed to each other's solo albums and all four Beatles appeared on Ringo's *Ringo* album in 1974, albeit on different tracks.

Any chance of a Beatles reunion ended on 8 December 1980 when John Lennon was murdered outside his New York apartment.

In 1995 McCartney, Harrison and Ringo came together to make the *Anthology TV* series and a 6-CD set that featured unreleased songs, studio out-takes and rare recordings from across their career as well as two unfinished Lennon songs over which they recorded to create two 'reunion' songs.

George Harrison became the second Beatle to die when he succumbed to cancer on 29 November 2001 in Los Angeles.

Proof of the enduring fascination with the Beatles came in late 2021 with the release of *Get Back*, an eight-hour, three-part documentary by Peter Jackson that went back to the 60 hours of film shot for the *Let It Be* movie and created an enthralling fly-on-the-wall account of the Beatles rehearsing and recording, culminating in their final rooftop concert.

'The Beatles will go on and on, on those records and films and videos and books ... and in people's memories. ... The Beatles, I think, exist without us.'

George Harrison

Further Information

Beatles Vital Info

John Lennon

Birth Name: John Winston Lennon

Birth & Death Dates: 9 October 1940–8 December 1980

Birthplace: Liverpool, England

Role: Singer, guitarist, songwriter

Paul McCartney

Birth Name: James Paul McCartney

Birth Date: 18 June 1942

Birthplace: Liverpool, England

Role: Singer, bass player, songwriter

George Harrison

Birth Name: George Harrison

Birth & Death Dates: 25 February 1943–
29 November 2001

Birthplace: Liverpool, England

Role: Guitarist, singer, songwriter

Ringo Starr

Birth Name: Richard Starkey

Birth Date: 7 July 1940

Birthplace: Liverpool, England

Role: Drummer, singer, songwriter

Discography

Albums

Release	Title	UK chart position	Weeks in chart	US chart position	Weeks in chart
Apr 1963	Please Please Me	1	70	-	-
Nov 1963	With The Beatles	1	51	-	-
Feb 1964	Meet The Beatles	-	-	1	27
Feb 1964	Introducing... The Beatles	-	-	2	26
Apr 1964	The Beatles' Second Album	-	-	1	26
Jun 1964	The American Tour With Ed Rudy	-	-	20	9
Jul 1964	A Hard Day's Night	1	38	1	14
Aug 1964	Something New	-	-	2	28
Dec 1964	The Beatles Story	-	-	7	9
Dec 1964	Beatles For Sale	1	46	-	-
Jan 1965	Beatles '65	-	-	1	38
July 1965	Beatles VI	-	-	1	21
Aug 1965	Help!	1	37	1	33
Dec 1965	Rubber Soul	1	42	1	39
Jul 1966	Yesterday And Today	-	-	1	15
Aug 1966	Revolver	1	34	1	24
Dec 1966	A Collection Of Beatles Oldies	7	34	-	-
June 1967	Sgt Pepper's Lonely Hearts Club Band	1	148	1	63
Jan 1968	Magical Mystery Tour	31	2	1	30
Dec 1968	The Beatles	1	22	1	25
Feb 1969	Yellow Submarine	3	10	2	12

Oct 1969	*Abbey Road*	1	81	1	32
Mar 1970	*Hey Jude (compilation)*	-	-	2	17
May 1970	*Let It Be*	1	59	1	20

Singles

Oct 1962	'Love Me Do'	17	18	1	11
Jan 1963	'Please Please Me'	2	18	3	10
Apr 1963	'From Me To You'	1	21	-	-
Jun 1963	'My Bonnie'	48	1	26	2
Aug 1963	'She Loves You'	1	31	1	14
Dec 1963	'I Want To Hold Your Hand'	1	21	1	14
Jan 1964	'I Saw Her Standing There'	-	-	14	8
Mar 1964	'Can't Buy Me Love'	1	14	1	9
Mar 1964	'Twist And Shout'	-	-	2	9
Apr 1964	'Do You Want To Know A Secret'	-	-	2	9
Jun 1964	'Ain't She Sweet'	29	6	19	7
Jul 1964	'A Hard Day's Night'	1	13	1	12
Aug 1964	'And I Love Her'	-	-	12	7
Sep 1964	'Matchbox' / 'Slow Down'	-	-	17	5
Dec 1964	'I Feel Fine'	1	13	1	11
Feb 1965	'Eight Days A Week'	-	-	1	9
Apr 1965	'Ticket To Ride'	1	12	1	9
Jul 1965	'Help!'	1	14	1	12
Oct 1964	'Yesterday'	-	-	1	9
Dec 1965	'Day Tripper' / 'We Can Work It Out'	1	12	1	11
Mar 1966	'Nowhere Man'	-	-	3	9
Jun 1966	'Paperback Writer' / 'Rain'	1	11	1	10
Aug 1966	'Yellow Submarine' / 'Eleanor Rigby'	1	13	2	8
Feb 1967	'Penny Lane' / 'Strawberry Fields Forever'	2	11	1	9
Jul 1967	'All You Need Is Love'	1	13	1	9
Nov 1967	'Hello Goodbye'	1	12	1	10
Dec 1967	'Magical Mystery Tour' (2-EP)	2	12	-	-
Mar 1968	'Lady Madonna'	1	8	4	10
Sep 1968	'Hey Jude'	1	16	1	19

Apr 1969	'Get Back'	1	17	1	12
June 1969	'The Ballad Of John And Yoko'	1	14	8	8
Nov 1969	'Something' / 'Come Together'	4	12	1	16
Mar 1970	'Let It Be'	2	9	1	13
May 1970	'The Long And Winding Road'	-	-	1	10

Beatles Record-Breakers

Most consecutive No. 1 hit singles in the UK: 11 between 1963 and 1966

Most Christmas No. 1 singles: 4

Most No. 1 albums in the UK: 15

Most weeks at No. 1 in the UK album charts: 175

First album to debut at No. 1 in the UK album charts: *Help!*, 1964

Most weeks at the top of the UK album and singles charts simultaneously: 45

Most consecutive weeks at the top of the UK album and singles charts simultaneously: 7

The biggest domination of the UK charts: In December 1963 for three consecutive weeks, The Beatles had the No. 1 and No. 2 top singles, the No. 1 and No. 2 top EPs and the No. 1 and No. 2 top albums

Most No. 1 hits in the US: 20 between 1964 and 1970

The only act to occupy the Top Five singles positions in the US charts simultaneously: on 4 April 1964

The only act to have three uninterrupted consecutive No. 1 Hits in the US: 1964

Most No. 1 albums in the US: 19

Most albums simultaneously in the US Top 200: 14 (2014)

Most-Covered Beatles Songs

'Yesterday'

'Something'

'Eleanor Rigby'

'And I Love Her'

'Blackbird'

Online

thebeatles.com

The official site for all the latest news and information.
Register to get a newsletter.

beatlesbible.com

'Not quite as popular as Jesus' apparently, but the
constant barrage of information emanating from this site is
truly miraculous.

beatlesagain.com/breflib.html

The most comprehensive archive you will find on
the Beatles.

beatlelinks.net/forums/index.php

Beatles discussion forum, from the trivial to the obscure.

chartingthebeatles.net

The Beatles' music explored through infographics.

Biographies

Hugh Fielder

Hugh Fielder's life changed after he heard 'Please Please Me' early in 1963. It heralded a pop music revolution and led to a career in music journalism that has lasted more than 40 years, to the bemusement of his parents, who wondered when he was going to get a proper job (his daughters still do). He has written books on Pink Floyd, Genesis, Queen, The Police and Lady Gaga, and is a regular contributor to *Classic Rock* magazine. The Beatles remain the yardstick by which he judges all other acts in terms of creativity and success. To this day, whenever he hears a Beatles song, he can hum the next track on the album when it finishes.

Tony Bramwell

Tony Bramwell grew up in Liverpool with Beatles George, Paul and John. His life became intertwined with The Beatles, first working for Brian Epstein at NEMS and then for The Beatles at Apple, heading Apple Films, then later as the CEO of Apple Records. After The Beatles split, he became the UK's first independent record promoter, representing artists such as Bruce Springsteen and co-ordinating and promoting music for films, including Harry Saltzmann's James Bonds (such as Paul McCartney's 'Live And Let Die') and *Chariots of Fire*, *Dirty Dancing* and *Ghost*. He released his memoir on the Fab Four called *Magical Mystery Tours: My Life With The Beatles*, which has become one of the most popular books among fans and followers.

SEE, LISTEN, LEARN
Make it Your Own

See our books, journals,
notebooks & calendars at
flametreepublishing.com